RHONDA

SUCCEED
because of what you've been
THROUGH

WORKBOOK

learn how to acquire the five points of prosperity

Copyright © 2010 by Rhonda Sciortino

All rights reserved. This book may not be reproduced, in whole or in part, without written permission from the publisher, except by a reviewer who may quote brief passages in a review; nor may any part of this book be reproduced, stored in a retrieval system, or transmitted in any form or by any means, electronic, mechanical, recording or other, without written permission from the publisher.

First Printing: February 2011

ISBN: 978-0-9830921-1-7

Published by: N&SMG, Inc., P.O. Box 13175, Newport Beach, CA 92658

www.rhondasciortino.com

Printed in China

Cover & Interior Design: David Riley Associates
Newport Beach, CA
www.rileydra.com
Cover Photography: Svoboda Studios

ON A PERSONAL NOTE

It is my heartfelt desire that you use this workbook to take control of your life and in so doing, to create the life you want to live. Few people would have thought that this white trash ghetto girl would ever have grown up to be a business owner, to create employment, and to stimulate the economy around me by investing into my community and into the lives of others. But that's exactly what happened. And it can happen for you too IF you're willing to do the work necessary to change your life. This workbook is designed to do just that. Only you can do this work. It doesn't matter how you started. What matters is how you finish. Turn the page, change your life.

Rhonda

*This first three chapters of the book
are designed to start you thinking about bad
experiences and difficult people in a different
way. As you answer these questions, begin to
shift your focus from what people have done to
you to what they did for you. Yes, I said "for
you" because you CAN use unfairness
to motivate you to accomplish more
with your life.*

CHAPTER 1

LESSONS FROM ABUSE

1. I never planned to tell anyone about my childhood. I couldn't imagine the point of reliving an ugly, painful past. But because of abuse, neglect, abandonment, and other unfair circumstances, I realize that I was driven by a powerful force to be wanted and valued, to do something worthwhile, to fit in, to be liked, and to have all the things that were denied to me. Telling about my past has helped me to deal with it and to see the lessons I learned (good and bad) from my childhood.

   Describe your childhood as you remember it. Try to include incidents that are difficult to remember and to talk about with others.

   _____

   _____

   _____

   _____

   _____

   _____

2. Although I didn't realize how important it was at the time, one of the few good things about my childhood was when my grandfather would say to me, "You don't know anything important." My response to him was, "Oh, yes I do!" This gave me the opportunity to tell excitedly the "important thing" I had learned that day from the encyclopedia or whatever else I had read.

If you can, describe a "good thing" from your childhood.

3. During my childhood there were several questions that were going through my mind. Why was I alive? Was there a God? If so, what the heck was He doing while the weaker, smaller, and more vulnerable of us were being hurt by the bigger, stronger ones? How could I protect myself and get out of this alive? And the question that really burned inside of me, although I probably couldn't have verbalized it until much later, was this: What could I do to change my circumstances?

What are some of the questions or thoughts that went through your mind as you grew up?

_____
_____
_____
_____
_____
_____

4. Two of the lessons I learned from my childhood experiences were:

    Because of the weakness of my grandmother in accepting the abuse that she and I suffered, I determined never to be weak and timid, to never allow anyone to hurt me again.

    From the feelings of powerlessness and the awful hunger that I so often felt as a result of my grandfather controlling what food we were allowed to eat as punishment for what he considered wrongdoing, I developed the determination to always work and earn my own money so that I would never again be under someone else's control.

    What are some "lessons" you learned from your childhood? How do these "lessons" affect the way you act or react now?

    _____
    _____
    _____
    _____

5. As a result of the painful experiences of my childhood, I learned how to read people, how to sense when tension is increasing, how to ignore insults, and how and when to fight back.

   What are some of the things you learned from your difficult experiences?

6. Many of the lessons we learn as children in dysfunctional environments have to be reassessed, revised, or eliminated entirely. For example, when I was 4 years old, my grandfather began to teach me how to properly handle, use, and clean a firearm, but these skills didn't help me in my insurance career. In fact, talking about this aspect of my upbringing could have negatively influenced the way people thought of me.

   Which one of your "lessons" from childhood has to be reassessed, revised, or eliminated altogether?

   _____
   _____
   _____
   _____
   _____
   _____
   _____
   _____
   _____
   _____
   _____
   _____
   _____
   _____
   _____

7. To cope with the poverty that I lived in, I looked at magazines to try to picture life in a clean home with nice furniture, clothes and shoes that fit, plenty of food, and the privacy of a bedroom of my own. In the little closet that was "my room," I read books to imagine life like "normal" people lived. When I was beaten, I imagined my grandfather being overcome by a big, strong man who delivered me.

What coping mechanisms have you acquired to help you deal with painful situations?

8. What you've been through qualifies you to do what others find difficult. What can you do that others find difficult to do?

LESSONS FROM ABUSE

_____
_____
_____
_____
_____
_____

As you are reading the book and completing this workbook, collect pictures from magazines or draw pictures of things that you want in your future. Include pictures of occupations that you want, a family that you want, and material possessions that you want, such as a house, a car, a television, etc. Place these pictures in a folder. These pictures will be used as you read Chapter 11 to create a poster of your future goals.

There are lots of people in your life who have taught you something. Some lessons are valuable and some were the result of the other person's twisted thinking. Sort through what you've learned to keep what will help you achieve success and to discard what is of no use.

CHAPTER 2

LESSONS FROM OTHERS

1. In my view, there are five key elements of prosperity: health, joy, peace, good relationships, and financial stability. Everyone who achieves all five elements of true prosperity must do what is necessary to have each of these things in his/her life. They are not obtained through luck or coincidence. Doing what is necessary to have a life that includes these aspects is what I call "paying your dues."

    What are some things you can do to "pay your dues" to have each of the five points of prosperity?

    a. Health (For example, eat healthy food and walk every day):

    _____
    _____
    _____
    _____
    _____
    _____
    _____

b. Joy (For example, choose to smile regardless of the circumstances): _____
_____
_____
_____
_____
_____
_____

c. Peace (For example, decide not to take offense when someone says or does something hurtful): _____
_____
_____
_____
_____
_____
_____

d. Good relationships (For example, look for a way you can help someone, expecting nothing in return): _____
_____
_____

_____

_____

_____

_____

_____

e. Financial stability (For example, think of a way you can earn some extra money or spend less today): _____

_____

_____

_____

_____

_____

_____

2. From my typing teacher, Mrs. Moyer, I learned how to type at 100 words per minute and take shorthand notes at 120 words per minute, which lead me to be hired and trained as an insurance customer service representative. This gave me opportunities to sit in on meetings where I learned things that I would not otherwise have had access to. I also learned a strong work ethic – how to give 100% of your effort to your job even when you don't feel like it – especially when you don't feel like it. I learned

the importance of looking people straight in the eye when you are talking to them. Finally, I learned the importance of faith in God.

What are some things that you have learned from your teachers or other supervisors?

3. Because of my experiences and what dysfunctional people tried to teach me, I believed that all romance novels are bad, that people with red hair are mean, that men who wear pinky rings should not be trusted, and that rich people are bad people. I discarded these beliefs when I realized that they were not true.

What are some beliefs that you have about people that probably should be questioned or reevaluated?

4. Name two people who have influenced you – for good or for bad.

   Person:_____

   What have you learned from him/her? _____

   _____
   _____
   _____
   _____
   _____
   _____
   _____

   Person:_____

   What have you learned from him/her? _____

   _____
   _____
   _____
   _____
   _____
   _____
   _____

5. Are there any "lessons" you learned in adolescence that will not serve you and could hinder your future success?

6. Which lessons that you have learned from others and from pain helped to create the good qualities that you have?

*You may have already worked through
a lot of issues and accomplished much in your
life. As you know, though, as long as you're
breathing, you can learn more. And the more you
learn, the more you're able to achieve.*

CHAPTER 3

LESSONS AFTER I THOUGHT I KNEW EVERYTHING

1. I couldn't wait to apply for emancipation to be on my own. When I was 15, I applied, saw a judge, and was sent away with a list of tasks to complete. This included:

   a. getting a job

   b. finding an apartment that I could afford

   c. getting a driver's license

   d. obtaining transportation

   e. maintaining good grades

   f. opening a checking and savings account

   There were at least six ways that I earned money to help me meet these requirements.

   a. an insurance telemarketing job

   b. tutoring kids in English and algebra

   c. bathing stinky dogs at a kennel

   d. selling blankets that I knitted or crocheted

   e. working at a shoe store

   f. painting houses

What are two ways of earning income that you can do or have done?

a. _____

_____

_____

_____

b. _____

_____

_____

_____

2. Although being emancipated did give me a sense of control over my life, the one thing that remained the same was that I felt so alone. In my young adolescence, I didn't realize that there are lots of people who feel a deep sense of loneliness, such as those who are dealing with an ugly medical diagnosis, a cheating spouse, financial problems, kids on drugs, the death of a loved one, or any other serious issue people face alone.

Name some people or types of people whom you know who face their problems alone.

a. _____

b. _____

c. _____

d. _____

WHAT UNFAIR CIRCUMSTANCES CAN MOTIVATE YOU TO ACHIEVE MORE?

3. At my first two job experiences, I had to deal with sexual harassment. I learned that even in situations where you are a good employee and doing the best job you can, you may still be faced with unfair circumstances – sometimes because of someone else's wrong behaviors. In my third job, the company replaced me while I was hospitalized with a difficult pregnancy. Again, this was an unfair circumstance that would be considered illegal in today's workplace. When I searched for my next job opportunity, I made sure that I was assertive, that I was ready for the job interview, and that I communicated clearly to the owner how much he and his company needed what I had to offer an employer. As a result of all of these experiences, I learned what I needed to know to start my own company and have greater control of my destiny.

What are some lessons you have learned from your job experiences?

_____

_____

_____

_____

_____

_____

4. What are the strong characteristics of your personality that will help you succeed? (For example, ambitious, determined, assertive, confident, tenacious, good listening skills, good communication skills, not easily offended, able to get along with everyone)

_____

_____

_____

_____

_____

_____

_____

_____

_____

_____

_____

_____

_____

_____

_____

_____

_____

_____

_____

5. Because of your experiences (not despite), whatever they are, you have a maturity, wisdom, and compassion that you couldn't learn in any other way. Because of the pain you have endured, you have a set of coping skills that are in direct proportion to what you have gone through. Someone who has never developed the coping mechanisms to handle tough times simply will not be able to function and succeed at things that you can do well.

What life lessons have you recently learned?

_____

_____

_____

_____

_____

_____

_____

_____

_____

_____

_____

_____

_____

_____

_____

*The first step to obtaining the five key
points of prosperity – good health, good
relationships, peace, joy, and financial stability
– is to take responsibility, effective immediately,
for the quality of your life.*

CHAPTER 4

WHY WE DO WHAT WE DO

Consider your beliefs. They are affecting your actions. It may be that some of your beliefs were the result of bad things that happened to you or from the adoption of someone else's twisted beliefs. Decide now, as an adult, what you are going to believe. And while you're doing this, give yourself a break. Forgive yourself for anything you think you did wrong when you were too young to know what else you could have done.

1. What are some conclusions that you have drawn about people based upon your difficult experiences? (For example, no one can be trusted; no one wants me; I am worthless.)

_____

_____

_____

_____

_____

_____

_____

_____

2. Our personalities get wounded when we are hurt as little children – both emotionally and physically – and sometimes we "heal crooked," which means that our personality is distorted. What childhood hurts caused you to "heal crooked"?

___
___
___
___
___
___
___
___
___
___
___
___
___
___
___
___
___
___

3. What are the "crooked places" in your personality? (For example, using the skills of manipulation to protect yourself or feeling that you deserve the mistreatment caused by others)

_____
_____
_____
_____
_____
_____
_____
_____
_____
_____
_____
_____
_____
_____
_____
_____
_____
_____
_____
_____

4. With what you know now, how can you straighten out the "crooked places" and draw more mature conclusions?

5. How has your personality been damaged by people who hurt you or by mistreatment from others? (Are you short-tempered? Do you overreact when something goes wrong? Are you overcommitted to do things to avoid disappointing others? Do you use food, nicotine, alcohol or drugs to medicate your pain?)

6. What does it mean to "be yourself"?

7. Do you frequently think about or talk about the bad, ugly, or unfair things that have happened to you? When was the last time you did this? How many times did you talk about the past last week?

8. I never wanted to repeat the mistakes made by my parents and grandparents – I didn't want to repeat the past. Although I had desperately sought approval as a child, I had never received it or saw it modeled, and I didn't know how to give it to my daughter. If my daughter got all A's and a B, I focused on the B. I criticized her and pressured her to do better, regardless of how well she had done. I never showed any appreciation for all the wonderful characteristics of her personality or applauded her efforts. I focused on trying to improve her, just like my grandfather always tried to improve me.

How have you repeated or recreated the past?

_____

_____

_____

_____

_____

_____

_____

_____

_____

_____

_____

_____

9. What rejection have you experienced and how is it affecting you now?

10. What can you do today to focus your attention on the needs of someone other than yourself?

TREATING PEOPLE RIGHT AND MAKING RIGHT CHOICES GETS EASIER AS YOU MATURE. MATURITY PRECEDES COMPLETE HEALING. HEALING IS NECESSARY FOR TRUE HAPPINESS.

The people who hurt us took something from us. Every minute more that you think about the words and actions that caused the hurt is another minute you're giving away. Begin now to get over the hurt and avoid being hurt again by deciding to move beyond those hurtful experiences. I realize it sounds simplistic, but I've done this. I know it works. YOU, and only you, choose what you will think about and say. Choose to think about good things, positive things. If there are none from your past that you can recall, create good things in your future that you dwell on.

CHAPTER 5

GET OVER THE HURT AND AVOID BEING HURT AGAIN

1. What hurtful event or experience do you frequently think about?

___

2. Write down how you would change that experience by imagining the memory differently. (For example, if you have a memory of being beaten by someone, imagine a big, strong person walking in and stopping this person or imagine that you get away from the abuser.)

_____

_____

_____

_____

_____

_____

_____

_____

_____

_____

_____

_____

_____

_____

_____

_____

_____

3. On a separate piece of paper write down a painful experience that frequently haunts your mind or influences your present thinking or behavior. When you are through, tear it into tiny pieces and flush it down the toilet. Flush the memory away with the paper.

4. If you fail to forgive someone who hurt you, what will happen to you emotionally and physically?

_____
_____
_____
_____
_____
_____
_____
_____
_____
_____
_____
_____
_____
_____
_____

5. On a separate piece of paper, write down the names of two people who have hurt you and write down how they hurt you. Truly, fully forgive those people for what they have done to you. This doesn't mean that you have to remain in relationship with them. Sometimes the best we can do is move on after forgiving people so that we aren't continually reminded of the past.

6. Recall a time when someone's actions made you feel hurt or angry. What might that person have been going through that would explain (not excuse) his/her behavior?

DECIDE TODAY NOT TO TALK ABOUT THESE HURTFUL EXPERIENCES OR THE PEOPLE WHO CAUSED THEM UNLESS IT IS WITH SOMEONE WHO IS HELPING YOU GET OVER THE HURT.

7. Name one hurtful person who is currently in your life and write down how you can avoid being around that person or change the type of interaction with that person.

Person:_____

How will I avoid him/her: _____
_____
_____
_____
_____
_____
_____
_____
_____
_____
_____
_____
_____
_____

8. Name three things that you can do when someone upsets you or mistreats you.

   a. _____

   b. _____

   c. _____

9. You are more likely to be hurt by people who have been hurt themselves. If you have been hurt before, you may be more vulnerable than someone who had a great childhood. If this is your situation, it's doubly important that you be very careful to avoid getting into close personal relationships with people who are more likely to hurt you. To help you better predict who is "unsafe" to be around, here are some of the characteristics that hurt people exhibit:

   - They are unpleasant to be around.
   - They use their past or their pain as an excuse for bad behavior.
   - They frequently talk about themselves and their issues.
   - They are jealous of other people or what they have (jealousy is a sign of insecurity).
   - They get angry easily and frequently.
   - They are often depressed.
   - They are vulgar.
   - They are immature and act childishly.
   - They act pitifully so that people will know they are hurting in the hopes that people will ask about their feelings, giving them an opportunity to talk about their problems.

   Which of the characteristics of hurt people listed above do you exhibit?

   a. _____

   b. _____

   c. _____

   d. _____

10. Which of these characteristics will you begin today to eliminate from your life?

   a. _____

   _____

   _____

   _____

   b. _____

   _____

   _____

   _____

   c. _____

   _____

   _____

   _____

   d. _____

   _____

   _____

   _____

11. What are three ways to avoid being hurt?

   a. _____

   _____

   _____

   _____

   b. _____

   _____

   _____

   _____

   c. _____

   _____

   _____

   _____

WHAT ARE YOU HOLDING ON TO?

12. Whenever I wondered if my mother or father ever thought about me on my birthday, sadness would overtake me. I would walk around at work with tears in my eyes, withdraw from friends, lock myself in my room and tell my little girl, "Mommy doesn't feel like playing right now." I'd usually wind up with a migraine headache or an upset stomach.

What are some negative reactions that you have whenever you think of the painful past?

_____
_____
_____
_____
_____
_____
_____
_____
_____
_____
_____
_____
_____

FORGIVE, FORGIVE, AND DID I MENTION, IT'S IMPORTANT TO FORGIVE? FORGIVING PEOPLE WHO HURT YOU IS NOT FOR THEM. IT'S FOR YOU.

13. One of the things that I did to forget the painful past was to think every day about what I wanted in my future. To help me with this, I cut out pictures from magazines of a Mercedes SL, a house on the beach, and a beautiful place to vacation. I glued them on poster board and looked at them first thing in the morning and the last thing at night. This wasn't an "empty exercise." I eventually had everything on that poster board.

    What are some things that you can do to forget your painful past?

    _____
    _____
    _____
    _____
    _____
    _____
    _____
    _____

IF PEOPLE ARE ALWAYS HURTING YOUR FEELINGS OR IF YOU OFTEN FIND YOURSELF UPSET AND OFFENDED OR ANGRY, A BIG PART OF YOUR PROBLEM MAY BE YOU.

14. Name three negative emotions, such as anger, depression, and tension, and ways to deal with them.

   a. _____

   b. _____

c. _____

_____

_____

_____

_____

15. What are some ugly things that you have said to someone or about someone else?

_____

_____

_____

_____

_____

_____

_____

_____

_____

_____

_____

_____

SURROUND YOURSELF WITH POSITIVE PEOPLE AND AVOID NEGATIVE PEOPLE.

16. If you surround yourself with positive people, what impact will this have on you?

___
___
___
___
___
___
___
___
___
___
___
___
___
___
___
___
___
___

17. If you surround yourself with negative people, what impact will this have on you?

18. Name three characteristics of people who are not safe to be around.

    a. _____

    b. _____

    c. _____

19. Many of the kids in my neighborhood were the only so-called friends that I knew as a child. But as time went on, many of them did not make good choices. One of them was shot execution style for using the drugs he agreed to sell. One is mentally ill because of her choice to destroy her brain with drugs. One was convicted of murder. One joined a gang by passing a gang's "entrance requirement" of shooting an innocent person. Another had a baby when she was 15 years old. Because they spent time together, they influenced each other. Therefore, all of the bad choices that they made seemed "normal" for them.

    Life turned out differently for me because of the decisions I made. I chose to work all day and study at night. I chose to do side jobs when I could find them and to wear the same clothes to work two or three days of every week. I chose to take my lunch rather than spend money on fast food. I chose to never smoke cigarettes or use drugs. During the time when I was making sacrifices for my future, many of the people I grew up with chose to smoke dope, live on welfare, complain, and feel sorry for themselves.

Who are the people in your life who are not making success-oriented choices? What bad decisions are they making? (Choose now to distance yourself from these people so that they don't hold you back from achieving success.)

20. If you must be around negative people, you have to work to balance the effect of their negativity in your life. Do this by listening to an audio book on positive thinking or anything that is uplifting. Turn off any television, music, or video that has any negative, ugly, or vulgar connotation to it because this is influencing your thoughts, words, actions, habits, character, and ultimately your future – whether you think it does or not. You will eventually say and do the things you see and hear because they will seem normal to you.

What are some things that you can do to counterbalance the effect of negative people and influences in your life?

_____

_____

_____

_____

_____

_____

_____

_____

_____

_____

_____

_____

FORGIVENESS, BY DEFINITION, IS UNDESERVED.

21. Which of the survival techniques listed in Chapter 5 have you used in order to deal with bad relationships? What other survival techniques have you used?

_____
_____
_____
_____
_____
_____
_____
_____
_____
_____
_____
_____
_____
_____
_____
_____
_____
_____
_____
_____

DON'T ALLOW OTHERS TO MISTREAT YOU.

22. Name two things that people tend to do when they are mistreated.

   a. _____
   b. _____

> *When people say or do something that hurts your feelings, or when they fail to do or say something that you wish they would do or say, don't assume that they're inconsiderate or intentionally trying to hurt you. Ask yourself, "What are they going through that would make them act the way they did?"*

23. List six characteristics or qualities that you want your spouse and closest friends to have.

   a. _____
   b. _____
   c. _____
   d. _____
   e. _____
   f. _____

List six characteristics or qualities that you would like your co-workers, neighbors, or friends to have. (Since these are important to you, work on developing them in yourself. You'll find that once you exhibit these qualities, you'll attract people to you who exhibit these same qualities.)

a. _____
b. _____
c. _____
d. _____
e. _____
f. _____

24. List five things that you are NOT willing to "put up with" in a relationship.

a. _____
b. _____
c. _____
d. _____
e. _____

YOU BECOME LIKE THE PEOPLE WITH WHOM YOU SPEND TIME.

25. Read the list of ways to develop a good relationship in Chapter 5.

    Which things do you currently do?

    _____
    _____
    _____
    _____
    _____
    _____

    Which ones do you need to focus on so that your relationships will improve?

    _____
    _____
    _____
    _____
    _____
    _____

26. What are you going to do within the next 24 hours to improve your relationships with family, friends, neighbors, or co-workers?

DO SOMETHING TO HELP YOURSELF AND QUIT HURTING YOURSELF.

27. In what ways are you hurting yourself with drugs, alcohol, nicotine, or junk food?

_____
_____
_____
_____
_____
_____
_____
_____
_____
_____
_____
_____
_____
_____
_____
_____
_____
_____

28. What other things do you do that you know you shouldn't do?

29. What can you do this week to quit hurting yourself?

You might have been the victim of someone else's bad choices, but as of today you are no longer anyone's victim. You don't need anyone's pity. You have everything you need to begin to take charge right now.

CHAPTER 6

TAKE CHARGE!

In order to have your new vision of yourself become a reality, you must first "take control" of your thoughts, your attitude, your words, and your actions. Don't automatically assume you cannot do it or that it is too hard. You CAN do this. And every time you change a thought, change a word, or change an action, you are actively changing your life!

GET CONTROL

1. What image do you now have of yourself – physically, emotionally, financially, socially?

   Physically: _____

   _____

   Emotionally: _____

   _____

   Financially: _____

   _____

   Socially: _____

   _____

2. How do you want to see yourself in these four areas?

   Physically: _____
   _____

   Emotionally: _____
   _____

   Financially: _____
   _____

   Socially: _____
   _____

3. One of the first ways that I lost control was when I became addicted to drinking 2 six-packs of Coca-Cola every day. One day I decided to take control of this addiction – I had my last soda. I had to take control of this trivial thing before I could take control of the big things in my life.

   What part of your personal life do you want to take control of and change?

   _____
   _____
   _____
   _____
   _____
   _____

_____

_____

_____

_____

_____

_____

_____

_____

4. I became disheartened at my job when I felt that I was being treated unfairly by my employer. The managers gave newly hired men choice sales leads and offered them better compensation programs. They were paid to attend conferences to help them find new clients. They were provided with customer service assistants to help them with their clerical tasks while I was expected to do this work myself. I had NO CONTROL over this. But rather than resign myself to dwell on the unfairness, I decided TO TAKE CONTROL. On May 3, 1989, I started my own business.

What can you do to take control of the way you earn an income and how much money you earn?

_____

_____

_____

_____

CONTROL YOUR THOUGHTS

5. If you want to change your future, you must change your _____.

    To change your character, you must change your _____.

    To change your habits, you must _____.

    To act differently, you must _____.

    To speak positively, you must have _____.

6. While I was being beaten as a little girl, I learned that I could endure being beaten if I "chose my thoughts." I would close my eyes and see something in my mind that was different than the surroundings of the situation, which helped to block out the pain and the sounds.

That coping mechanism helped me to focus on something other than whatever pain or discomfort I was feeling in the workplace or in my personal relationships. I could push through the pain and get to work when I didn't feel like it. I had the ability to think about something else when co-workers were talking about me behind my back or when supervisors passed me over for an opportunity I thought I deserved.

List five positive thoughts that you can choose to have about yourself.

a. _____

b. _____

c. _____

d. _____

e. _____

f. _____

7. Give an example of what you should do if a negative thought comes to your mind.

_____

_____

_____

_____

_____

THE POWER OF WORDS

8. At the age of 8, a man who was my neighbor told me that I would be a millionaire by the time I was 30. These words stuck in my mind, and by the age of 30, indeed I was a millionaire.

   What predictions about your life have you heard from other people? (Positive or negative)

What positive predictions can you make about yourself and your life?

_____
_____
_____
_____
_____
_____

9. When I had to do without something that I needed for myself and my daughter (i.e., food, clothes, furniture), I'd say to her, "I don't have money for it now, but one day we will be able to buy anything we want." Those words ultimately became a reality.

Give an example of some negative words that you have said to yourself. Then rewrite those statements in a positive way.

Negative words that you've said to yourself:

_____
_____
_____
_____
_____
_____

Positive way to describe this situation:

ACTIONS AND HABITS

10. What positive things are you known for doing? (For example, being happy, being organized, always working, always looking good)

11. What negative things are you known for doing? (For example, complaining all the time, gossiping, being moody or angry)

12. What do you want to be known for doing?

ELIMINATE BEHAVIORS THAT DON'T FIT THE NEW YOU.

13. For survival in my tough neighborhood, I carried a knife, had a foul mouth, and walked with a swagger, all of which was intended to show that I wasn't intimidated by anyone in my neighborhood. I had to eliminate those behaviors because they did not fit the person I wanted to be. Walking around like a "tough guy" doesn't work in a professional environment. I had to turn that tough talk and attitude into an attitude of confident assurance – and be careful not to allow it to be perceived as arrogance. Had I failed to file the rough edges off, I wouldn't have lasted long in the professional world.

What coping mechanisms and behaviors from your childhood have to be eliminated because they no longer fit the person you want to be?

_____

_____

_____

_____

_____

_____

_____

_____

14. When my "friends" didn't ask me to join them in some of their activities, I acted like I wasn't interested in participating. In some cases, I went so far as to say they were losers and I didn't want to be around them. When I revised that "coping mechanism" of acting as though I didn't want to be invited anyway into choosing not to be offended or hurt, I eliminated opportunities for more pain. Ultimately, I adopted the attitude that if someone didn't invite me, it was surely just an oversight. I deliberately chose to refuse to be offended.

What coping mechanisms and behaviors from your childhood would be useful to you as an adult, but they need to be refined or revised?

_____

_____

_____

_____

_____

_____

_____

_____

_____

_____

15. List the seven character traits of people who have lasting, genuine prosperity.

    a. _____

    b. _____

    c. _____

    d. _____

    e. _____

    f. _____

    g. _____

16. Name someone you know or know of who has persevered in spite of having failures and difficult experiences, and describe how he/she has persevered.

    Person: _____

    How has he/she persevered? _____

    _____

    _____

    _____

    _____

    _____

    _____

    _____

17. What can you take charge of right now?

"GO from broke to prosperous." Success will not come to you. You have to go to it. The most brilliant and talented person in the world will achieve nothing if he/she stays in bed all day. It's not until we get up, get out, and actually DO the proven steps to success that we'll achieve anything. A person with a good attitude and willingness to do the work will achieve more than the most intelligent person who chooses to do little or nothing. Yes, I said "choose." Doing nothing is a choice.

CHAPTER 7

PREPARE YOURSELF FOR SUCCESS

Success will not just show up in your life. You have to do your part to earn it. Preparation for success is necessary. Begin today to change your mind, your words, and your actions to prepare yourself for your success.

1. I was prepared for success on my first job because in high school I invested a lot of time and energy in learning and practicing the skills that I was taught. I worked hard to be able to type accurately at 100 words per minute and take shorthand at 120 words per minute so that I was ready when the job opportunity that required these skills presented itself.

    What did you do (or are you doing) to prepare yourself for success?

    _____
    _____
    _____
    _____
    _____

2. Even after I emancipated, I pictured myself as a white trash ghetto girl, which telegraphed to successful people that I was not prepared to receive success.

   Are you picturing yourself negatively, which shows people that you are not prepared to receive success? If so, how?

3. After modeling the behavior of many mentors, I eventually dropped the label of "white trash ghetto girl." The first major change came when I chose to emulate "church ladies." These ladies seemed nice and approachable, never got into a conflict, were always pleasant and positive, and had a reputation of helping others. I was also watching and listening to my boss, a very successful business man. I began to read the books he read, to say the kinds of things he said, and to act the way he did with clients. And to learn how to dress and groom myself professionally, I listened to the advice of two of my insurance clients, one of whom was a hair stylist who cut my hair into a more professional look and helped me buy more appropriate clothes.

Name two role models who have what you want, and list the things that you learned from these role models. Remember, you don't have to know these people. They can be people you know of or have read or heard about.

Role Model #1: _____

What did you learn from him or her? _____

_____

_____

_____

_____

Role Model #2: _____

What did you learn from him or her? _____

_____
_____
_____
_____
_____

ACT LIKE YOUR ROLE MODELS UNTIL YOU BECOME YOUR OWN "CUSTOMIZED" COMPILATION OF ALL THE THINGS THAT YOU ADMIRE IN OTHERS.

4. Of the four famous "world changers" listed in Chapter 7, which one do you admire the most and why?

_____
_____
_____
_____
_____
_____
_____
_____

5. Who is another famous person you admire and why?

_____
_____
_____
_____
_____
_____
_____
_____
_____
_____
_____
_____
_____
_____

HOW DO YOU COME UP WITH YOUR "MILLION DOLLAR IDEA"? PAY ATTENTION TO PEOPLE'S PROBLEMS AND COME UP WITH A SOLUTION WITH BROAD APPEAL.

Everything that you have experienced in your life has made you the person you are and has prepared you for your unique purpose. There is meaning to your life. It's your responsibility and obligation to find it. When you consider the clues of who you are, the desires of your heart, the things that bug you, and the solutions to the problems of others, your unique purpose will begin to come into view.

CHAPTER 8

YOU'RE HERE FOR A REASON

1. The skills that you used to survive adversity have built up a strength in you that others don't have. Of the eight skills listed at the beginning of Chapter 8, which ones apply to you?

   _____
   _____
   _____
   _____
   _____
   _____
   _____
   _____
   _____
   _____

2. Many of the bad things that happened to me during my childhood prepared me for the work that I currently do and motivated me to be successful. For example, because my grandparents lost what little we had in a fire due to lack of insurance when I was

8 years old, I learned the importance of insurance, which gave me a passion for protecting people with appropriate insurance coverage. Had I not experienced the feeling of having nothing and being hungry, perhaps I wouldn't have taken the risk to open my own business. I figured that I'd been hungry before and worked my way into a good job, so I could do it again if this business didn't make it. If I hadn't been abandoned by my parents, abused by my caregivers, and experienced a brief time in foster care, I wouldn't have the passion I feel today for protecting people and organizations that care for abused children.

If I hadn't had all these experiences, I would never have taken the leap of faith and opened my own insurance business focused solely on protecting people and organizations that care for vulnerable youth and their families. Had I not taken that leap, I never would have helped pave the way for a change in rating insurance premiums for homes for abused children that has resulted in millions of dollars in savings annually for children's homes across the country.

What specific difficult experiences have you had that have prepared you for the workplace?

_____

_____

_____

_____

3. What are some childhood experiences that could squash or destroy a person's creativity?

WHO ARE YOU?

To identify your purpose and the unique set of talents, skills, and abilities that have been planted inside of you, use the pages at the back of this workbook to write out the answers to the following questions. Answers to these questions are some of the clues to discovering your purpose and the "assignment" you are uniquely qualified to accomplish.

1. What are the qualities that you like best about your personality?

2. What comes easily to you? What do you do well?

3. What do you know something about? What do you know more about than the average person?

4. What bugs you? What can you do to change it?

5. What are you interested in?

6. What opinions and judgments do you have that influence your decisions, actions and thoughts?

7. What would you do if you weren't afraid?

8. Is there something you would do if you knew you couldn't fail?

9. What do people come to you for? (For example, to get advice, to listen to their problems, to get a laugh, to do them a favor)

10. What compliments did you receive as a child? An adolescent? Now?

11. What is the result of your creativity?

12. What makes you laugh?

13. What are your favorite talents, skills, or abilities?

14. What were your nicknames as a child? An adolescent? Now? (positive or demeaning)

15. What should your nickname be now? (positive only)

16. What are your daydreams?

17. What heroic feats have you performed?

18. What quality have you most improved since becoming an adult?

19. What things come out of your mouth on a regular basis? (What are you known for saying? What would you like to be known for saying? These are clues to what you "stand for.")

20. List all the reasons you should congratulate yourself.

21. What is the funniest joke you've ever told or the best practical joke you've ever pulled?

22. If you had to summarize your life into a motto or slogan, what would it be? (This may be the same as what you'd like to shout out loud to friends, family, co-workers, and everyone else you meet. These are more clues to what you "stand for.")

23. List the warnings/advice you heard as a child.

24. List the character traits or actions that helped you through the tough times in your life.

25. What advice would you give to a young person about to reach adulthood?

26. What's your best advice to a person getting married?

27. What advice would you give to someone about to have his/her first child?

28. What advice would you give to the parent of a child with health or behavioral difficulties?

29. What advice would you give to someone opening his/her own business?

30. What advice would you give to someone with a terminal illness?

31. What do you know for sure? (How is it different from what you knew when you were younger? How do you think it might be different 25 years from now?)

32. List the things you want to do before you die. (If you're bold, set timelines on each of these.)

33. List the most exhilarating experiences you've ever had.

34. List the places, people and things you've seen that altered your view of the world.

35. What were the difficult experiences of your life, and what lessons did you learn from them?

36. List the beliefs you'd go out on a limb for.

37. List the people you'd step in front of a bullet to protect.

38. What were the biggest turning points in your life?

39. How have you sabotaged yourself? (Or how do you hold yourself back from what you really want?)

40. What people have changed your life for the better? How?

41. What positive contributions have you made in this world?

42. What words (and from what person) do you long to hear?

43. Is there someone longing to hear something from you? If so, what is it and what is holding you back from saying it?

44. What traits do you value in your friends?

45. What inspires you to keep going when you get discouraged?

46. What do you want your obituary to say?

47. What miracles do you know have happened?

48. What things in nature remind you of your connection to the "big picture"?

49. What's wrong with most people nowadays?

50. If you suddenly received $10 million dollars and were told you must spend it to help others, how would you spend it?

REFLECTION: WHO ARE YOU?

a. As you think about your answers and your recollections while considering the answers to these questions, is there anything about yourself that surprises you? If so, what?

b. What clues do the answers to all these questions give you about yourself and what you are uniquely designed to be able to accomplish?

Every truly successful person makes right choices and treats people right. Once you become accustomed to this way of living, it comes so naturally that you don't have to even think about it. Make no mistake; this is not an option. This is necessary to the achievement of all five points of true prosperity.

CHAPTER 9

MAKING RIGHT CHOICES AND TREATING PEOPLE RIGHT

1. When we are unsure of what to do, we have to check our choices against the decisions that we think our role models would make.

   How can your mentors be helpful when you make choices?

   _____

   _____

   _____

   _____

   _____

2. List five examples of things that you can do to treat people right.

   a. _____
   b. _____
   c. _____
   d. _____
   e. _____

3. What are examples of three consequences of choosing not to treat people right?

   a. _____

   b. _____

   c. _____

4. What are three rewards of treating people right?

   a. _____

   b. _____

   c. _____

5. Describe an incident where you did not treat people right that resulted in or contributed to a negative outcome.

   _____
   _____
   _____
   _____
   _____
   _____
   _____
   _____
   _____
   _____
   _____

6. Now rewrite the above incident to show how you could have treated people differently and enjoyed a more favorable result.

_____
_____
_____
_____
_____
_____
_____
_____
_____
_____
_____
_____

IT'S IMPORTANT THAT YOU MAKE RIGHT CHOICES AND TREAT PEOPLE RIGHT, ESPECIALLY WHEN YOU DON'T FEEL LIKE IT. WHEN YOU LEAST FEEL LIKE DOING THE RIGHT THING IS WHEN IT WILL BENEFIT YOU MOST!

Whether you are an employee or a business owner, serving others is the key to success. Follow the guidelines for work in Succeed Because of What You've Been Through *and they will literally change your life.*

CHAPTER 10

SERVING OTHERS IS THE KEY

1. Regardless of whether you hate your job, can't stand your boss, are ridiculed by your coworkers, are treated harshly by customers, or generally are mistreated, if your employer is paying you, you must do the best job you can for the time you have sold to your employer.

   Do you consider yourself to be a good employee or a bad employee? Why? _____

   _____

   _____

   _____

   _____

   _____

   _____

   _____

   _____

   _____

2. If all of your assigned work has been completed at your job, what are some things that you could do to make good use of your time?

___

SHARE PERSONAL PROBLEMS AND GOALS ONLY WITH PEOPLE YOU CAN TRUST. PEOPLE WHO HAVE NO ULTERIOR MOTIVE OR PERSONAL INVESTMENT IN THE OUTCOME OF THE SITUATION OTHER THAN YOUR WELL-BEING.

3. How can you keep a negative working environment from affecting you?

4. How can you help to create a positive working environment?

5. If you have a valid complaint about something in the workplace, what is the best way to voice your complaint?

6. What should you do if you are unavoidably late to work, miss a deadline, or make a mistake?

   _____
   _____
   _____
   _____
   _____
   _____
   _____
   _____

7. Name three things that you should not expect from your job.

   a. _____
   b. _____
   c. _____

8. What are some good reasons to ask for a raise?

   a. _____
   b. _____
   c. _____
   d. _____

9. How can you make yourself one of the most knowledgeable employees about your company?

_____
_____
_____
_____

10. Name five other ways that you can become a more valuable employee.

   a. _____
   b. _____
   c. _____
   d. _____
   e. _____
   f. _____

11. Why is it so important to have a good attitude on the job?

_____
_____
_____
_____
_____
_____
_____

12. Describe a person you know who has a bad attitude in the workplace.

___

13. Describe a person you know who has a positive attitude in the workplace.

___

It's been said that what gets measured gets done. If you don't specifically set goals, you'll never reach them. No one passionately pursues a vague aspiration. Work this section to set specific goals until you can clearly see them in your imagination.

CHAPTER 11

SO WHAT DO YOU WANT?

Improving your life requires making a decision to have goals, setting specific goals in each area, determining the price you will have to pay to achieve each goal, and then paying the price.

1. Before you set a goal, you should research the available options. What are some resources for researching your options?

   _____
   _____
   _____
   _____

2. What are some options for you in setting a goal?

   a. For your health? _____
   _____
   _____

   b. For your relationships? _____
   _____
   _____

c. For your career? _____

_____

_____

d. For your home? _____

_____

_____

3. Although I originally wanted to be a lawyer, I decided against this career after some research. I learned that the daily life of the kind of lawyer I aspired to be included long hours and lots of stress, followed sometimes by not getting the conviction you thought should result from all that hard work. I discovered that there would be years of expensive law school after completing my bachelor's degree. This research caused me to give up my goal because I was not willing to pay the price. Don't be reluctant to change your goals when new information leads you to new conclusions.

All of us tend to dream about a career in our childhood that is not realistic. What is an unrealistic career that you once wanted as a child?

_____

_____

_____

_____

Why does that career seem unrealistic to you now?

4. Why is it so important to write down a plan and timelines for achieving your goals?

LOSERS FOCUS ON WHAT THEY'RE GOING THROUGH. WINNERS FOCUS ON WHAT THEY'RE GOING TO.

5. What are some things that tend to distract us from achieving our goals?

6. I've experienced many setbacks in business. Early on, I would work for months without pay, hoping to make the sale, only to have the prospect choose another option. A major setback was when an employee stole a credit card from my purse and charged furnishings for an office she was opening to compete with me! Another time I spent thousands of dollars putting together an insurance company deal that was to be exclusively mine. Eventually, the insurance company gave the program to another broker, and the program I helped to create became my competition.

Name four things that you should do when obstacles arise or setbacks occur.

a. _____

b. _____

_____

_____

_____

c. _____

_____

_____

_____

d. _____

_____

_____

_____

7. Of the seven typical excuses listed in Chapter 11 for not achieving your goals, which ones are you more likely to use as an excuse?

_____

_____

_____

_____

_____

_____

8. Set some short-term goals:

   a. What do you want to change by next week? _____
   _____
   _____
   _____
   _____

   b. What do you want to have changed one month from now? _____
   _____
   _____
   _____
   _____

   c. What do you want to have achieved six months from now? _____
   _____
   _____
   _____
   _____

d. What do you want to have achieved one year from now?

_____

_____

_____

_____

9. What do you want to do with your life? Set some long-term goals – goals that you plan to achieve twenty years from now.

Goal #1: _____

_____

Goal #2: _____

_____

Goal #3: _____

_____

Goal #4: _____

_____

NEVER GIVE UP

10. Are you really committed to doing what is necessary to achieve each one of your goals? What will you have to do?

_____

_____

USING THE PICTURES THAT YOU HAVE BEEN COLLECTING, CREATE A POSTER OF YOUR GOALS.

11. What are you afraid of happening that might keep you from achieving your goals?

SO WHAT DO YOU WANT?

IF YOU ARE NOT DOING SOMETHING YOU LOVE, FIND SOMETHING YOU DO LOVE TO DO AND FIGURE OUT HOW TO MAKE A LIVING AT DOING IT.

Dare to imagine how you will feel when you have the things you want. Gather the information, get the facts, and know your options now so that when money starts showing up, you won't get overwhelmed and make bad decisions.

CHAPTER 12

MAKE MONEY WORK FOR YOU!

1. Our attitude about money acts as an important variable in whether or not we have it, have enough of it, handle it responsibly when we get it, and keep it long-term. So,to get to the point that you have enough of it to accomplish all your goals, you must overcome any attitudes that may keep you from getting money and keeping it.

What beliefs do you have about people who are wealthy?

_____
_____
_____
_____
_____
_____
_____
_____
_____

2. In order to have enough money to pay for the education and other things I wanted my daughter to have, to buy a house, to invest in office buildings and warehouses, and to buy the cars, clothes, and other things I wanted, I made a lot of sacrifices. I delayed purchasing many things I wanted, such as new clothes, shoes, dinner out, furniture, and a nicer car, in order to save money so that I could invest in the things that would generate the money that would allow me to have the luxuries I wanted after having the basic needs met.

In what area of your life can you make a decision to spend money differently so that in the long run you can accumulate money to invest and eventually have what you really want?

_____

_____

_____

_____

_____

_____

_____

_____

_____

_____

_____

3. When I was in my early 20's, I multiplied what money I had with the help of partners. For example, I asked the owner of a junkyard, a mechanic, and a paint and auto body man if they would be interested in a partnership. We bought "theft recovery" cars from the junkyard and fixed them up. My role was to advertise and sell the finished product. We were a group of four with each person contributing what he/she had or knew how to do. Only one was contributing cash, the junkyard owner. Everyone made a good return on his/her investment, which was a revenue stream for each of us in addition to the wages from our employment.

With the profits from sold vehicles, we began to purchase houses, fix them up, and sell them for a profit. This allowed people who didn't have very much money to get involved in purchasing a property that they could not otherwise afford.

What ideas do you have to multiply what money you have?

_____

_____

_____

_____

_____

_____

_____

4. Using the guidelines that are given in Chapter 12, what are some things that you can do in the future to help you purchase a car or any other "big-ticket item" wisely?

5. When is it wise to use credit to purchase something?

THERE MAY BE TIMES WHEN YOU ARE TRYING TO BUY SOMETHING THAT IS A CRITICAL PART OF THE ACHIEVEMENT OF YOUR GOALS AND YOUR REQUEST FOR HELP IS TURNED DOWN. WHEN THIS HAPPENS, DON'T GET DISCOURAGED, ANGRY, OR DEPRESSED. JUST KEEP TRYING. IF YOU DON'T GIVE UP, YOU WILL SUCCEED!

6. How can you diplomatically ask someone for exceptions in order to achieve your goals?

_____
_____
_____
_____
_____
_____
_____
_____
_____
_____
_____

7. When you have accumulated money, there are more ways to multiply your money. List four of these options.

   a. _____

   b. _____

   c. _____

   d. _____

8. In what way can a wealthy person be compared to a farmer?

   _____
   _____
   _____
   _____
   _____
   _____
   _____
   _____
   _____
   _____
   _____
   _____
   _____
   _____
   _____

9. If you need a partner in order to achieve your goals, what traits and skills would you want your partner to have?

_____

_____

_____

_____

_____

_____

_____

_____

_____

_____

10. List the six things that you should do if you have a conflict with your partner.

a. _____

b. _____

c. _____

d. _____

e. _____

f. _____

11. When I made slightly more than minimum wage, I did many things to "stretch my money." I looked for day-old bread, the dented cans, and the vegetables, fruit, and meat sold at half price. When I'd see a fruit tree with limbs full of fruit, I'd stop and ask if I could buy a bag of fruit for $1. (Most of the time, people told me to just take what I wanted.) I took my lunch to work, used coupons in grocery stores, drank tap water instead of soda, went to the movies in the afternoon instead of the evening, and sat on the floor with pillows rather than buying furniture. I bought Top Ramen, oatmeal, rice, beans, pasta, and peanut butter and created filling meals with these items. I learned how to sew and made clothes for myself and my daughter. I mailed in rebate forms and celebrated when the $1 rebate would arrive. When I needed a hair cut, I went to the local beauty college and paid a fraction of what others paid at the salon. I didn't buy anything that I didn't absolutely need.

List six things that you can do to keep more of what you earn.

a. _____

b. _____

c. _____

d. _____

e. _____

f. _____

Many people have achieved amazing success in their lives. Learn from them. It doesn't matter how you started in life. It matters how you finish.

CHAPTER 13

ADVICE OF ROLE MODELS

1. Name the three people from this chapter whose advice means the most to you.

   Person:_____
   Advice: _____
   _____
   _____

   Person:_____
   Advice: _____
   _____
   _____

   Person:_____
   Advice: _____
   _____
   _____

2. On the internet, search for advice from three people whom you admire the most. (For example, a pastor, a sports figure, a performing artist, a business person, or a politician)

Person you admire: _____

Why: _____

_____

_____

_____

_____

_____

_____

_____

Person you admire: _____

Why: _____

_____

_____

_____

_____

_____

_____

_____

ADVICE OF ROLE MODELS

Person you admire: _____

Why: _____

_____
_____
_____
_____
_____
_____
_____
_____
_____

I am delighted to say that I've paid my dues, and my life is now wonderful. It isn't perfect; there are still challenges. But having lived poor and wealthy, I can testify to the fact that it is infinitely easier to live with financial prosperity.

CHAPTER 14

THE PRESENT IS SO GOOD

1. Of the ten things listed in Chapter 14 that really count (in addition to money) in order to have genuine prosperity, which ones are the most important to you?

   _____
   _____
   _____
   _____
   _____
   _____
   _____

2. What are the most important things that you have learned from reading this book, *Succeed Because of What You've Been Through?*

   _____
   _____
   _____
   _____

_____

_____

_____

_____

_____

_____

_____

THINGS YOU CAN DO IMMEDIATELY TO IMPROVE YOUR SITUATION THAT REQUIRE NO MONEY AND LITTLE TIME

1. Look in the mirror and smile many times throughout every day. Initially you'll have to force yourself to remember to do this. Set a goal of a minimum of 20 times every day. Eventually, you will incorporate a genuine smile into your countenance without any effort. I am aware of how nutty and inconsequential this sounds, but if you will do this, you will see how very effective this can be in changing your attitude, your mood, the people around you, and the outcomes of situations you find yourself in. In a way, smiling through the most difficult of situations is evidence of faith that you believe the difficult situation will pass and that things will get better. It's a self-fulfilling prophecy!

2. Say to yourself, "I like myself!" a minimum of twenty times every day. This is even more powerful if you look in the mirror

while doing this. I dare you to do this without smiling. I don't think it can be done! If you do this seemingly silly, insignificant thing, you'll find yourself in a better mood. Why? Because you're undoing the negative effects of unkind words said to and about you before you were able to sift through them and devalue or discard them.

3. LAUGH! Remind yourself of things that make you laugh. Watch a funny movie or television show. Get a book of jokes. Figure out what it takes to make you laugh, and then make a concerted effort to do that. The world is so serious that we have to be deliberate about lifting our mood. Laughter truly does make you feel better. No, it doesn't fix everything, but regardless of what you're going through, your life will be easier to deal with if you have a smile on your face and some laughter in your heart.

4. Make a list of your positive characteristics. Be sure to include the positives of your personality and character in addition to your appearance. Then remind yourself of these characteristics every day. What you're doing is paying yourself a compliment! For example, say, "I am one of the most resourceful people I know!" Or "I am resilient – a strong survivor." Or "I can get along well with just about anyone." "I'm honest and trustworthy." "I'm a good worker and have good work ethic."

5. Put your past and your future into perspective by creating a timeline.

PUTTING THINGS INTO PERSPECTIVE

In this exercise, you will create a timeline of the significant events of your life from birth to present. Make a brief notation of specifics at the ages when life-altering events transpired.

As an example, here is mine:

AGE	EVENT
Age 6 mo.	Abandoned
Age 4	Burned
Age 6	Taken to Mother, Mother Refused
Age 9	Visited Father
Age 14	Met Barbara Moyer
Age 16	Emancipated
Age 17	Married
Age 17	Insurance License
Age 19	Baby
Age 21	Hired by Fred
Age 22	Met Corky Kindsvater
Age 27	Started Business
Age 30	Married Nick Sciortino

Create your timeline of life-altering events:

AGE	EVENT

GETTING FOCUSED ON THE FUTURE

In this exercise, you will create a timeline of the significant events of your life from today until the last day of your life. Make a brief notation of specifics at the ages when you would like your future life-altering events to transpire.

Include things like getting married, having children, getting the education you desire, obtaining the job you want, receiving the income you aspire to earn, starting your own business, or anything else on your goal list.

As an example:

AGE	EVENT
Age 18	Now
Age 23	College Degree
Age 23	Start Career as a Nurse
Age 25	Get Married
Age 27	Purchase Home
Age 28	Have Children
Age 36	Purchase Rental House
Age 40	Teach Nursing Classes
Age 42	Buy BMW
Age 50	Purchase Retirement Home in Colorado
Age 55	Trip to Europe
Age 60	Trip to China
Age 65	Retire In Colorado

Create a timeline of your future:

AGE	EVENT

If you keep these two timelines in a prominent place where you will be reminded regularly of what you've been through and what you wish to achieve, you will grow in your resolve to reach your goals and in your confidence in yourself to attain them!

PROMISE YOURSELF

I believe that one of the reasons that I was able to overcome some of the unfairness and adversities I faced as a child was that I made promises to myself along the way. I encourage you to make some promises to yourself now:

- I take responsibility for my thoughts.
- I take responsibility for my words.
- I take responsibility for my attitude.
- I take responsibility for my behavior.
- I am in control of my life.
- I am in control of my money.
- I am in control of my attitude toward my relationships.

What other promises do you want to make to yourself?

Sign and date this and make sure you keep your promises.

Signature: _____

Date: _____

I've told you about my success, and it will be an immeasurable joy for me to hear about your success. As you make progress, log onto www.rhondasciortino.com and tell me about it so I can celebrate with you!

SUCCEED BECAUSE OF WHAT YOU'VE BEEN THROUGH

SUCCEED BECAUSE OF WHAT YOU'VE BEEN THROUGH

SUCCEED BECAUSE OF WHAT YOU'VE BEEN THROUGH

SUCCEED BECAUSE OF WHAT YOU'VE BEEN THROUGH

SUCCEED BECAUSE OF WHAT YOU'VE BEEN THROUGH

SUCCEED BECAUSE OF WHAT YOU'VE BEEN THROUGH